LET'S GO!

CARS

by Tessa Kenan

TABLE OF CONTENTS

D0680822

CARS

This car is small.

This car is big.

short

This car is short.

long

This car is long.

This car is old.

This car is new.

This car is slow.

This car is fast!

WORDS TO KNOW

fast

long

new

old

short

slow

INDEX